THE COOLEST CHINESE Artifacts

Jill Keppeler

NEW YORK

SinolinguA
华语教学出版社

BEIJING

Published in 2022 by The Rosen Publishing Group, Inc.
29 East 21st Street, New York, NY 10010

Jointly published in 2022 by Sinolingua Co.,Ltd., Beijing, China, and The Rosen Publishing Group, Inc., New York, New York, United States.

First Edition

Editor: Jill Keppeler
Designer: Rachel Rising

Photo credits: Cover, Leo McGilly/Shutterstock.com; cover, pp. 1–48 Sylfida/Shutterstock.com; cover, p. 1 CkyBe/Shutterstock.com; pp. 4, 6, 10, 14, 18, 22, 26, 30, 34, 38, 42 Somchai Som/Shutterstock .com; p. 5 Lou-Foto/Alamy Stock Photo; p. 7 https://commons.wikimedia.org/wiki/File:Pots,_Yangshao_culture,_neolithic_China,_c._2600-2300_BC,_ceramic_-_%C3%96stasiatiska_museet,_Stockholm_-_DSC09657.jpg; p. 8 Paul Atkinson/Shutterstock.com; p. 11 DnDavis/Shutterstock.com; p. 12 Hung Chung Chih/Shutterstock.com; p. 15 https://commons.wikimedia.org/wiki/File:Sword_of_Gou_Jian,_King_of_Yue_(9873583704).jpg; p. 16 Roy Chau/Alamy Stock Photo; p. 19 https://commons .wikimedia.org/wiki/File:Xia_Jade_Bi_Disc.jpg; p. 20 ZUMA Press, Inc./Alamy Stock Photo; p. 23 https://commons.wikimedia.org/wiki/File:Han_Woman%27s_Semi-Formal_Coat,_China,_1880-1889,_silk_-_Cincinnati_Art_Museum_-_DSC03147.jpg; p. 24 Mirko Kuzmanovic/Shutterstock.com; p. 27 https://commons.wikimedia.org/wiki/File:Luoshenfu_Gu_Kai_Zhi.jpg; p. 28 https://commons .wikimedia.org/wiki/File:Fan_K%27uan_001.jpg; p. 31 https://commons.wikimedia.org/wiki/File:Tian-tsui_(kingfisher_feather)_hair_pins.jpg; p. 32 https://en.wikipedia.org/wiki/File:Ming_Empress_Crown_b .jpg; p. 35 https://commons.wikimedia.org/wiki/File:Tang_dynasty_pottery_dumplings.jpg; p. 36 https://en.wikipedia.org/wiki/File:Teapot_(Yixing_ware,_about_1900).jpg; p. 39 https://commons .wikimedia.org/wiki/File:XingshuLantingxv.jpg; p. 40 Sumalee/Shutterstock.com; p. 43 feiyuezhangjie /Shutterstock.com.

Some of the images in this book illustrate individuals who are models. The depictions do not imply actual situations or events.

Cataloging-in-Publication Data
Names: Keppeler, Jill.
Title: The coolest Chinese artifacts / Jill Keppeler.
Description: New York : Rosen Young Adult, 2022. | Series: Crazy cool China | Includes glossary and index.
Identifiers: ISBN 9781499472455 (pbk.) | ISBN 9781499472462 (library bound) | ISBN 9781499472479 (ebook)
Subjects: LCSH: China–Antiquities–Juvenile literature. | Excavations (Archaeology)–China–Juvenile literature.
Classification: LCC DS715.K46 2022 | DDC 931–dc23

Manufactured in the United States of America

CPSIA Compliance Information: Batch #CSRYA23. For further information, contact Rosen Publishing, New York, New York, at 1-800-237-9932.

Contents

Pieces of the Past

Few regions around the world have flourished quite like China. Not only has this huge country been a world powerhouse for years, it also has thousands of years of recorded history, giving historians a better look at its past than most. And with that recorded history and all its detail come artifacts from throughout the centuries, pieces of the past that we can marvel at, wonder at, and study to learn more about this amazing culture.

In 2012, a team of Chinese and American scientists found a number of plain, brown pieces of pottery in a south China cave. These fragments were about 20,000 years old, which made them the oldest-known pottery in the world. The discovery led researchers to conclude that early people developed pottery much earlier than we used to think, even before they started to settle and developed agriculture.

Some Chinese artifacts are small, able to be studied as they're protected by museum display cases or showcased by photos online. Some, however, are huge, like the Great Wall, which stretches thousands of miles across the country even today. Some are everyday items, such as eating dishes, while some are rich with precious metals and gems. But no matter whether small or large, ordinary or precious, China's artifacts give us a valuable glimpse into its past.

Scientists used to think that ancient people didn't develop pottery until about 10,000 years ago. A discovery in China showed researchers otherwise!

The Power of Pottery

Pottery probably doesn't seem very cool. In fact, it might seem downright boring. However, it's such a common artifact that scientists can learn a lot from different kinds that they find in different places around the world.

Archaeologists have found examples of decorated pottery vessels from Mesolithic times, which were from about 10,000 to 5,000 BCE. In fact, these are the earliest examples of any Chinese art! They were decorated with **geometric** designs and markings from cords. By the

Archaeology is the study of human history using objects from that history. That's what artifacts are, in fact—objects that are portable, or can be picked up and moved, although sometimes larger things are also considered artifacts. Pieces of pottery are called potsherds, or just sherds. To archaeologists, the word "shard," although a very similar word, means something different. It means pieces of broken glass.

Neolithic time period, especially the middle to later stages, pottery was even more common and more decorated.

One particular Neolithic Chinese culture, the Yangshao culture, was centered around the Yellow River and actually called the "painted pottery" culture. Yangshao pottery was decorated with designs in colors that included red and black. However, many of these pots and jars weren't used for what you might think. People were buried in these jars! They were pretty much Yangshao coffins.

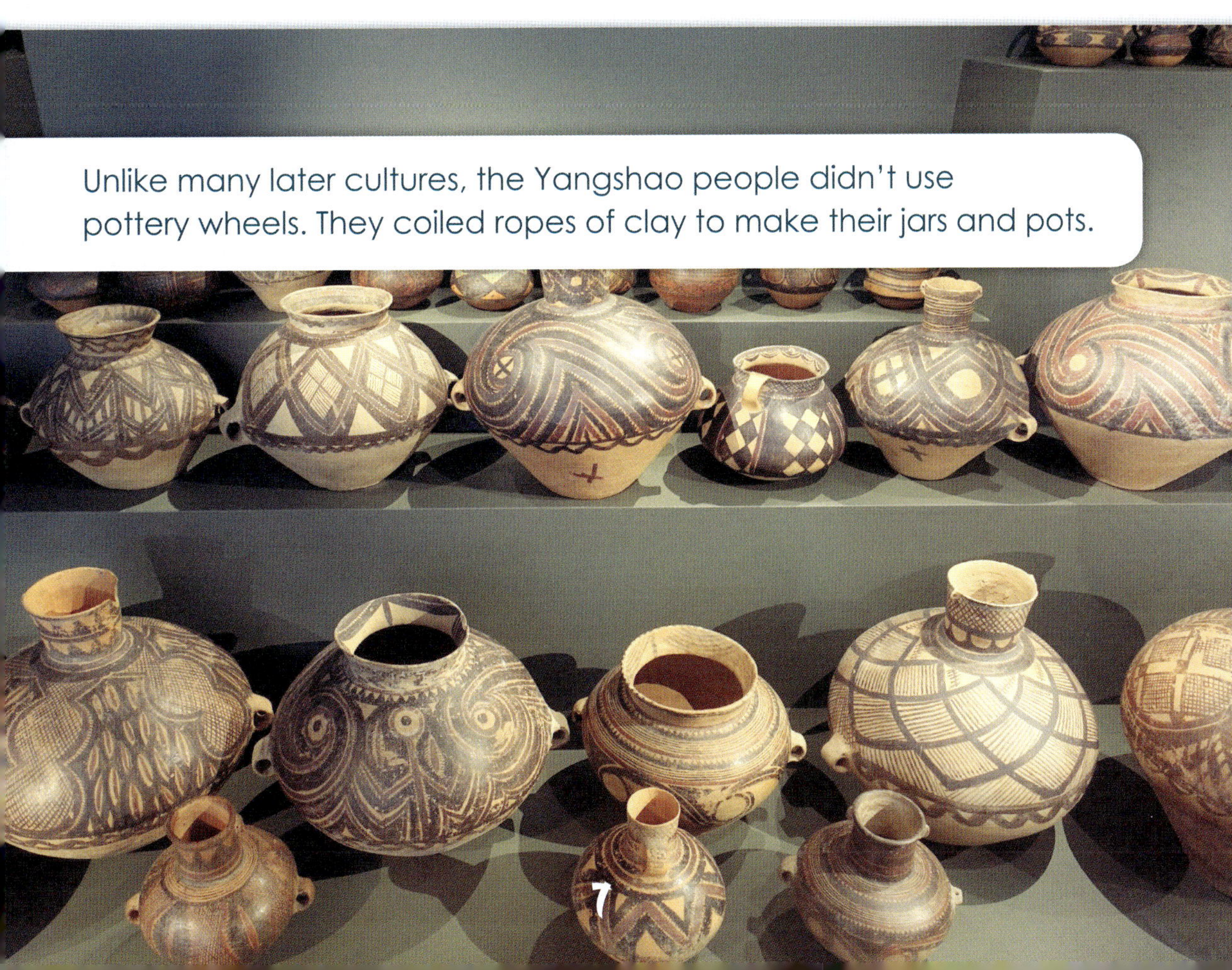

Unlike many later cultures, the Yangshao people didn't use pottery wheels. They coiled ropes of clay to make their jars and pots.

The Ming **dynasty** was in power from 1368 CE to 1644 CE. Porcelain from this time, often with blue-and-white patterns, may be the most famous of all Chinese pottery.

The Shang dynasty was the first Chinese dynasty to be historically verified in the modern day. It lasted from about 1600 to 1046 BCE. China has had many dynasties, but the most famous are likely the Shang, the Zhou (the longest-lasting dynasty at 789 years), the Qin, the Han, the Tang, the Song, the Yuan, the Ming, and the Qing. Many dynasties had their own distinct types of pottery and porcelain as methods and artistic techniques changed.

Once China was into its **Bronze Age**, following the Xia came the Shang dynasty—and pottery became more elaborate. This age brought the advent of Chinese porcelain. This is a sort of very fine pottery that's made by slowly heating certain kinds of clay. This type of pottery became a major export from China in the following centuries, and it influenced similar goods in many other places.

This was only the start. The Han dynasty is when truly large amounts of pottery began to survive for modern archaeologists to find. Colored glazes became more common during the Tang dynasty, and there was a notable increase in pottery technology during the Song dynasty. And to this day, Ming dynasty vases and other pieces (often with distinctive blue-and-white patterns) are worth a lot of money to collectors.

The Terracotta Army

The ancient Chinese didn't just use the wealth of clay in their region to make useful pottery (such as cups and plates) and fine porcelain (such as Ming vases). They sometimes made figures out of it as well. These figures could show humans or animals such as camels and horses. These were sometimes placed in tombs, with the belief that the dead person would be able to use what the figures represented in the afterlife. These were particularly popular during the Tang dynasty (618–907 CE).

The soldiers of the Terracotta Army are tomb figures placed to guard the tomb of the first emperor of China, Ying Zheng, who lived from 259 BCE to 210 BCE. Archaeologists think more than 700,000 people worked to build the tomb complex, which is at least 22 square miles (57 sq km).

However, the most well-known Chinese tomb figures aren't from the Tang dynasty—and they aren't small. In 1974, farmers digging a well near the city of Xi'an found something very unusual: a life-size clay soldier! The government sent archaeologists to the site, and they found something—or some things—even more extraordinary. There were thousands of clay soldiers (and their equally full-size clay horses) buried at the site!

Three of the biggest pits at the site where the terracotta soldiers were found are preserved in the Museum of the Terracotta Army, which was built right around that site.

Those who can't travel to China to see where the Terracotta Army was found can still see some of its soldiers. There are two traveling exhibits that showcase them.

Each soldier in the Terracotta Army is marked with the name of the foreman who oversaw its creation. It took 40 years or so for workers to complete the army. There were apparently crossbows rigged to shoot anyone who broke into the complex to rob it, although they haven't been found.

Each of the soldiers of the Terracotta Army has a unique expression on its face. Some still have colors from paint on the surface, although they're mostly grayish brown now. They carry swords, arrows, and other weapons. Their accompanying horses pulled bronze chariots. There may be as many as 8,000 figures.

However, we still don't know the full number, and we may never know. The tomb, including the emperor's burial chamber, hasn't been completely **excavated**. Some other pits around the tomb have yielded statues of dancers and acrobats, and writings from the Han dynasty say there are models of buildings within its walls as well.

By the Sword

Swords, like the ones found with the soldiers of the Terracotta Army, can be extremely cool artifacts. But probably the single coolest historic sword of all comes from China too.

In 1965, a team of archaeologists found a series of tombs in Hubei, China. In one, next to the skeletal remains of a body that had been buried there, they found an air-tight wooden box—and in that box, there was a 22-inch (56 cm) sword. The blade, sheathed in a black **scabbard**, was still sharp and free of **tarnish**. This was particularly amazing, not only because the tomb had been waterlogged for years, but

The sword of Goujian is made of tin bronze. This is an **alloy** made from tin and copper. It's harder than copper alone because of the added tin. In the case of this sword, it's mostly copper, with more tin along the edges. The tin helped keep the edges hard and sharp.

also because archaeologists believe the sword is more than 2,500 years old!

Historians dated the sword to a period from about 771 to 403 BCE. Markings on one side of the blade were identified as characters from an ancient script. Some of them were translated to mean "the king of Yue," and others suggested that the sword was

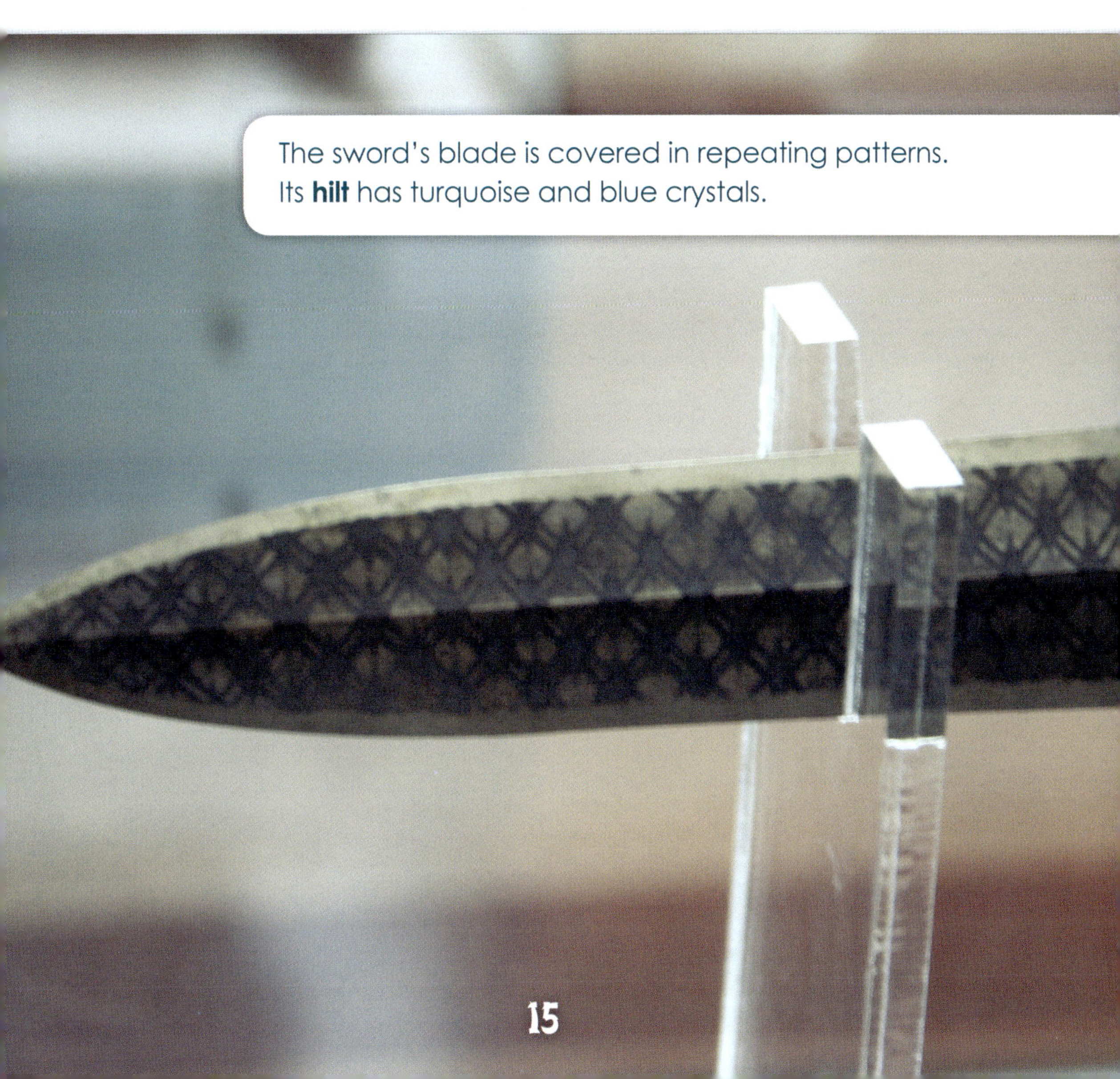

The sword's blade is covered in repeating patterns. Its **hilt** has turquoise and blue crystals.

The script on the sword of Goujian is called bird-worm seal script. The characters sometimes look a bit like birds and sometimes a bit like worms.

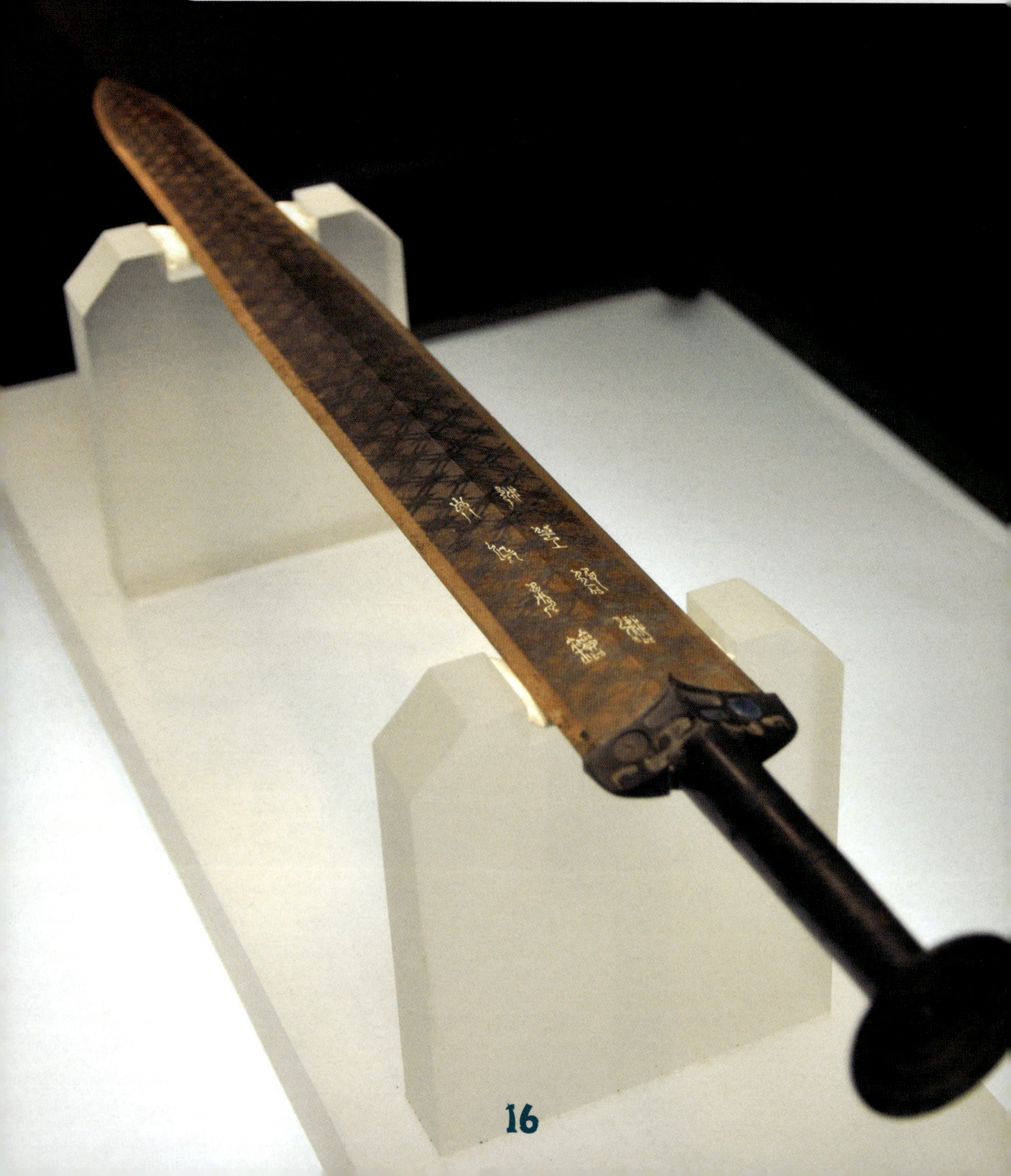

In 1994, the sword of Goujian was on loan to a facility in Singapore when a worker bumped the sword against its case. This caused a small (.27 inch, or 7 mm) crack in the blade. Today, the artifact isn't allowed out of China. It's considered a state treasure, and it's now on display in the Hubei Provincial Museum.

made for his personal use. Those studying the sword eventually identified Goujian as the king of Yue in question. He ruled from 497 to 465 BCE.

Goujian has an interesting story all on his own. He was king during a period of war, and he spent time as a prisoner of another king. Even during his time in freedom, he apparently led a simple life, sacrificing for his people and eventually bringing his kingdom to a time of victory and prosperity. And now, more than 2,500 years later, his name is still known around the world because of the fascinating history of one ancient sword.

Jade Culture

Ancient China is often associated with jade, a kind of gemstone that carves well, takes a high polish, and is often (but not always) connected with a deep green color. It's a very special material to the Chinese: not only valuable but also associated with moral virtues including loyalty, wisdom, and **integrity**.

There are actually two gemstones that have been called jade throughout history. One is jadeite, which is often considered to be worth more. The other is nephrite. The stone generally used in ancient Chinese jade art is nephrite, although jadeite and other minerals were sometimes used as well. It can be white, yellow, green, red, black, or any other color.

The earliest forms of jade art date to the Neolithic period. Much early jade sculpture was apparently related to burials. At some point in this period, people began carving the first-known examples of *bi* discs and *cong* cylinders, often out of jade. The discs, flat with a hole in the middle, were a symbol of heaven and believed to ward off evil. The *cong* was a cylinder or partial cone with a square exterior. These may have been **ritual** objects related to the earth.

As time went on, both *bi* discs and *cong* cylinders became more highly decorated. Archaeologists have found many examples of them in Chinese burial sites throughout the centuries.

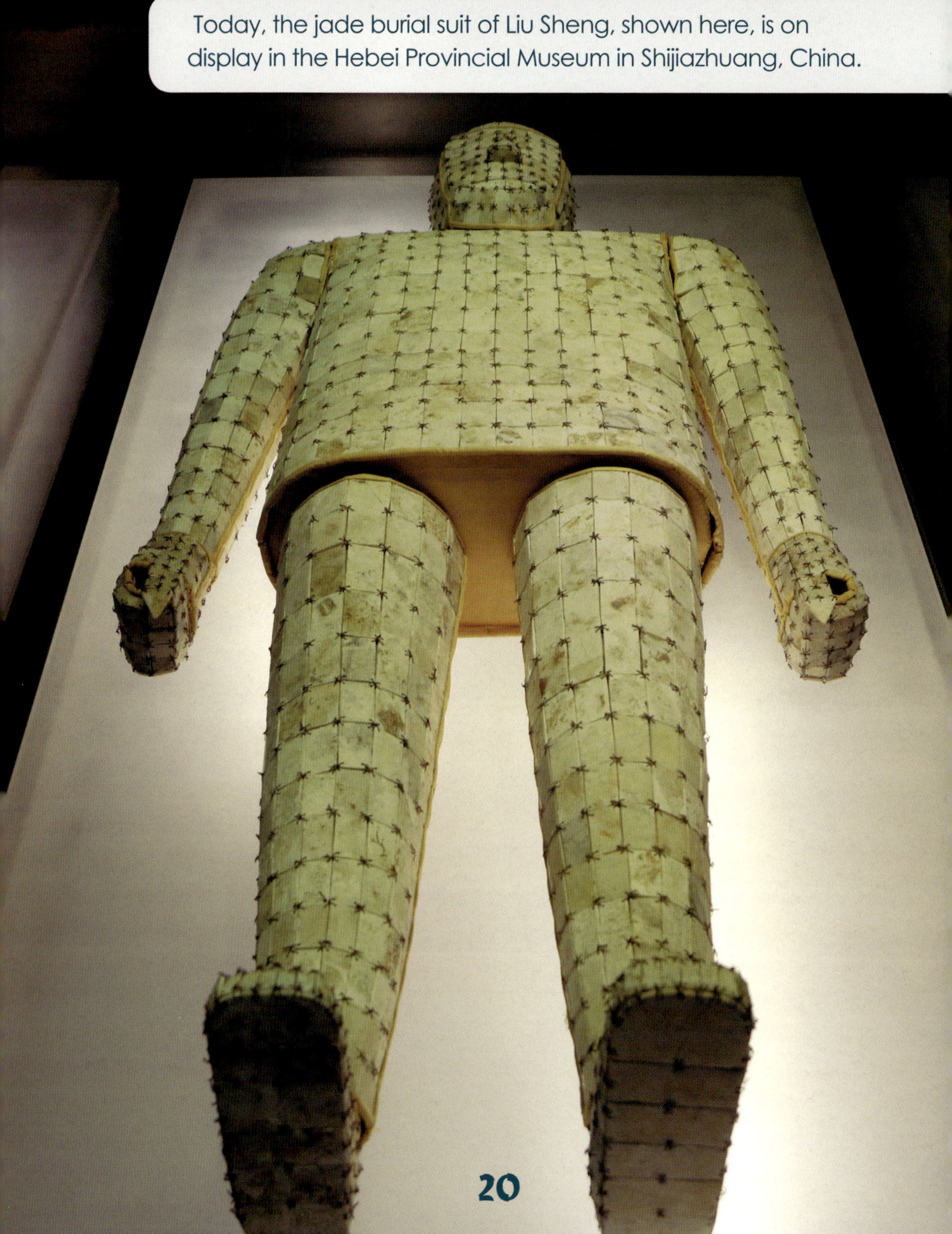

Today, the jade burial suit of Liu Sheng, shown here, is on display in the Hebei Provincial Museum in Shijiazhuang, China.

Jade was an important symbol to the Chinese, and so were dragons, who represented power, luck, and hope. So, it's not surprising that dragon figures carved from jade are another type of common Chinese artifact. The earliest discovered is sometimes called "The First Dragon of China." Dating to about 7,000 years ago, it's about 10.2 inches (26 cm) tall and now kept at the National Museum of China.

As China moved into the time of the Shang dynasty, jade carving became more elaborate, and the types of items varied more. Artisans made weapons out of jade (likely used for ceremonial purposes), masks, musical instruments, and human and animal figures. The use of the material continued through future dynasties, and it's still popular with artists today.

Perhaps one of the most notable (and unusual) uses of jade in dynastic China took place during the Han dynasty (206 BCE–220 CE). Researchers have found bodies from this period buried in suits made entirely of thin jade panels, sometimes tied with silver or golden thread. These include the bodies of Prince Liu Sheng and his wife, Princess Dou Wan, found in 1968 in their tomb in the Hebei Province. Each of their burial suits is made of more than 2,000 pieces of jade.

Smooth as Silk

China's even more well known for its silk cloth than it is for jade. Even the famous trade route linking China with the West was called the Silk Road, in part because of the amounts of silk cloth that China traded. How did this ancient relationship begin?

Silk is a fiber made by some insects and spiders and used to make webs and cocoons. In the case of the famous fabric, it's made by silkworms, the caterpillars of the moth species *Bombyx mori*. Their cocoons can be spun into thread and woven to make the fabric. For many years, only the Chinese knew how to make silk. Anyone caught trying to take the secret out of China could be put to death!

The earliest silk-related artifacts found in China weren't examples of the cloth itself. Archaeologists have found pottery models of silkworm cocoons and a real cocoon that had been cut in half. The earliest example of actual fabric was found in Henan, a province in China, and dates to 3630 BCE. After that, examples become more common—and more beautiful and elaborate.

Silk was very important to the Chinese. As a trade item, it could be worth its weight in gold. In fact, the government often used it in a way as a form of currency, or money. They gave it as gifts as a form of **diplomacy**. During some times, only royalty was allowed to wear clothing made of the fabric.

By the Han dynasty, silk was a major Chinese export. Many silk items, like this woman's coat, were works of art.

Dragon robes often have nine dragons and many other symbols on them.

Chinese stories say that the wife of the legendary Yellow Emperor (Huangdi) discovered silk. According to a tale told by Confucius, she was drinking tea while sitting under a mulberry tree when a silkworm cocoon fell into her cup. She realized that it was unraveling and that the material could be used to make thread. She went on to invent the loom used to weave silk cloth and taught all the people about her findings.

The Chinese developed many different techniques for working with the prized silk fabric, weaving it and decorating it in elaborate ways. Brocades are woven fabrics with a raised design, while damask is another sort of patterned fabric. The Chinese also used silk as a background for painting and writing for many nonwearable works of art.

By the Ming (1368–1644 CE) and Qing (1616–1911 CE) dynasties, silk garments were truly amazing art forms. Dragons were a popular **motif**. In fact, court dress items called "dragon robes" are some of the most beautiful examples of Chinese silk today. These robes feature woven dragons (including the imperial five-clawed dragon only the emperor was supposed to wear) and other special symbols. Many were very colorful and detailed.

For Art's Sake

While the ancient Chinese definitely made a lot of objects (everyday and otherwise) into works of art, they also produced art for, well, simply art's sake. Early examples of fine arts included paintings on cave and burial chamber walls. From the time of the Han dynasty, sometimes called the golden age of Chinese art, we have artifacts including sculpture (often used as tomb figures) and mural paintings (again, often in tombs).

By the 300s CE, there were a few surviving examples of the work of a man some call

The examples of Gu Kaizhi's work that survive today are on silk scrolls. Paper existed by this time in China (it was invented about 100 CE), but while the newer medium gradually took over in many ways, silk remained popular for painting and **calligraphy**. Scrolls could accommodate long paintings too. *Nymph of the Luo River* is about 10 inches (27.1 cm) tall by 225 inches (572.8cm) long! That's more than 18 feet (5.7 m).

the "founder of Chinese painting." Gu Kaizhi was born in Wuxi, China, and lived from about 348 to 409 CE. In addition to his painting, he was also a poet and a writer of works on painting theory. He wrote, "In figure paintings, the clothes and the appearances were not very important. The eyes were the spirit and the decisive factor."

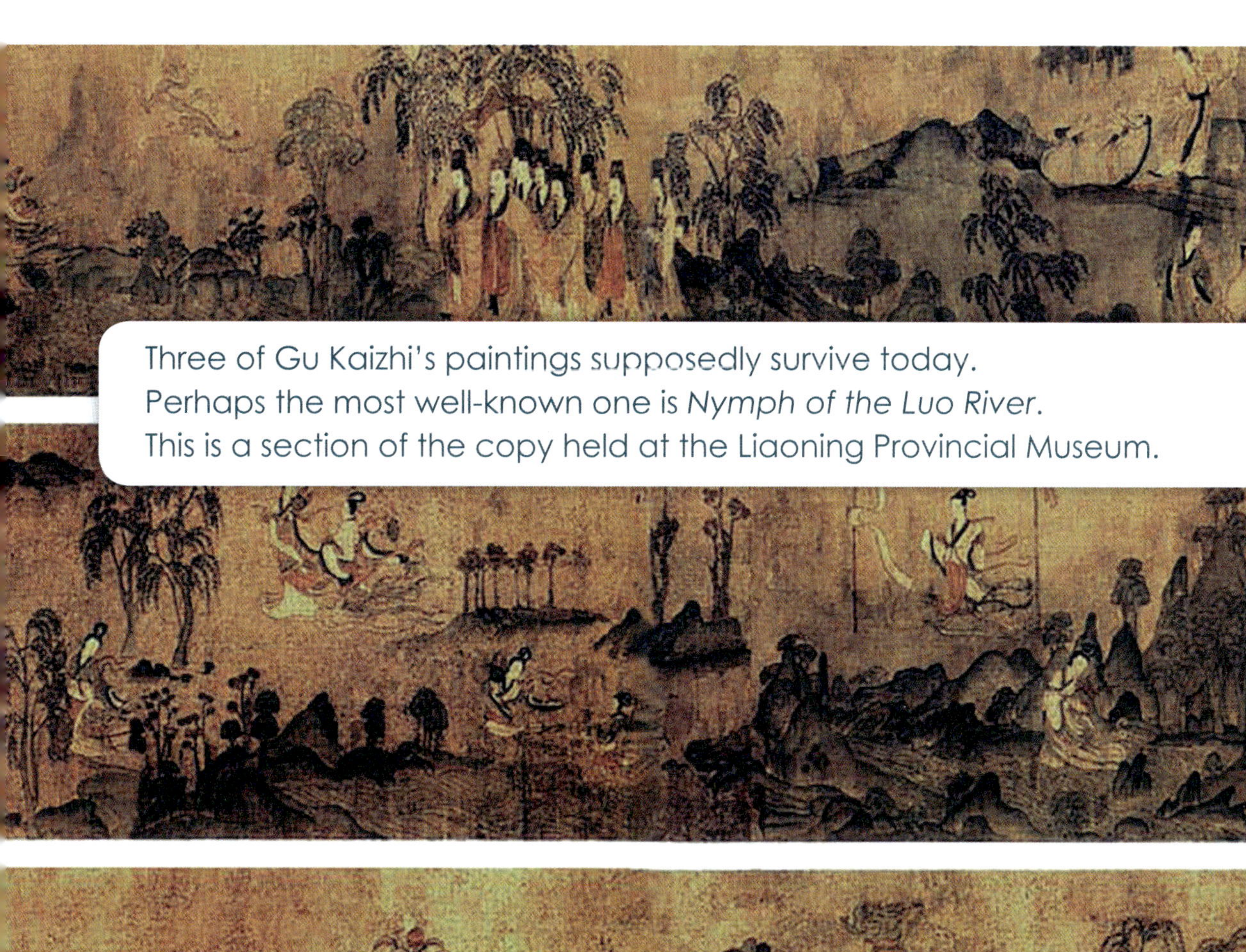

Three of Gu Kaizhi's paintings supposedly survive today. Perhaps the most well-known one is *Nymph of the Luo River*. This is a section of the copy held at the Liaoning Provincial Museum.

The painting *Travelers Among Mountains and Streams* by Fan Kuan, painted on silk, is known in part for how small the human figures of the painting look against the elements of nature.

The religion and philosophy of Daoism (also spelled "Taoism") has had a profound impact on Chinese life and culture, including art. Among other principles, Daoism emphasizes harmony with (and respect for) nature, and this philosophy is reflected in much Chinese landscape art, including the work of Fan Kuan and his contemporaries.

but it was landscape paintings that truly came to represent Chinese art. This type of painting first began to achieve great popularity during the Tang dynasty Tang dynasty (618 to 907 CE). This is also the time from which we start to have many Chinese painters' names. Wu Daozi is a Tang-era painter who influenced many later artists.

The Five Dynasties period (907–960 CE) and then the Northern Song dynasty (960–1127 CE) are considered particularly notable times in Chinese landscape painting. While there are dozens of painters known by name from this time period and after, one notable trio was made up of the so-called three great rival artists: Li Cheng, Fan Kuan, and Guan Tong. Not much of their original work survives, but there are copies and, like Wu Daozi, they influenced many later artists.

Jewelry with Meaning

Like silk clothing, personal items like jewelry can be art forms too—and the ancient Chinese had a flair for the **intricate** and elaborate in this form as well. They often used their beloved jade in these pieces, but that wasn't the only material. Jewelry also included gold or silver, or even what we might consider more ordinary materials, such as glass, stone, and clay. Men and women wore jewelry, which could include pins, rings, earrings, necklaces, hair ornaments, belts, and headdresses. Museums have many examples of these items, as many women in particular were buried with them.

One type of Chinese art with a somewhat tragic backstory is that of *tian-tsui*. In this, artists carefully cut up real kingfisher feathers—which are a stunning blue color—and glued bits to silver jewelry to create items of the same bright blue. This art form was common for thousands of years. However, people killed so many kingfishers for their feathers that the birds became endangered.

As with silk robes, dragons were a popular design, as were other mythological creatures, such as phoenixes. Pretty much everything had a meaning. Turtles meant longevity, or long life, as did the pine and crane. A couple of mandarin ducks meant a wish for a happy marriage. A lotus meant harmony.

Kingfisher feathers could give jewelry the look of cloisonné, or enameled metalwork. The Chinese also used forms of cloisonné for jewelry and to decorate other items.

This phoenix crown was found in the tomb of Empress Dowager Xiaojing, who lived from about 1565 to 1611.

In ancient Chinese culture, the dragon symbolized the emperor, while the phoenix symbolized the empress. A phoenix is a mythological bird that can be a sign of peace or a sign of rebirth. In mythology, it's considered female, so with the dragon (male in Chinese legend), the two together are a symbol of marriage and harmony.

Some of the largest and most elaborate forms of Chinese jewelry were headdresses, coronets, and crowns. In particular, the headdresses called *fengguan*, or phoenix crowns, are amazing works of art. Noblewomen or royalty would wear them for weddings or other official ceremonies from about the time of the Tang dynasty. The style was at its height during the Ming dynasty.

Phoenix crowns were not **subtle**—in fact, many were downright huge. They could include kingfisher feathers and thousands of gemstones and pearls. With all that decoration, they weren't light. A very elaborate crown could weigh 5 pounds (2.3 kg) or more! Imagine carrying a typical bag of flour around on your head all day.

Ultimate Leftovers

Studying artifacts can sometimes tell archaeologists what ancient peoples ate as well as what they wore and what art they cherished. Sometimes, though, this is more **literal** than in other times! The National Museum of China has on display actual dumplings made during the Tang dynasty, still preserved after about 1,700 years. Archaeologists found them in tombs buried in the Turpan, Xinjiang Uygur autonomous region in western China. The relatively good shape of the treats was likely due to the desert conditions in the area. Researchers could even tell that the dough was made of wheat flour and which ones had been stuffed with meat.

Many different cultures eat a type (or two, or three) of dumplings. These food items are made of a **leavened** dough that is boiled or steamed. In some kinds, the dough is stuffed with some sort of filling. The dough itself can also be flavored. Chinese culture has many kinds of dumplings, but two basic kinds are *gao*, which are crescent shaped, and *bao*, which are round.

Historians already knew that older peoples ate dumpling-type foods, in part because of old writings and in part because researchers found a buried wooden bowl full of dumpling-like objects in the same general location back in 1972. It was apparently part of grave goods intended to keep the deceased person supplied in the afterlife.

Eating dumplings is supposed to mean good luck for the new year. The 1,700-year-old ones probably shouldn't be consumed, however.

Teapots and other tools used to prepare tea can be artifacts too. Yixing clay teapots are made from a special sort of clay found in eastern China. This one dates from about 1900.

Tea is an important part of Chinese culture. Lu Yu, a writer during the Tang dynasty, wrote *The Classic of Tea*, about 760 CE. This is the first-known book on the subject—but it wouldn't be the only one. Tea was mentioned as one of the "seven necessities to begin the day," or of Chinese life in general, in other early works. Various forms of tea ceremonies have been around in China just about as long as the drink itself.

The ancient dumplings aren't the first or only time archaeologists have found a well-preserved item to let us know what our ancestors ate—or drank. They've also found evidence of tea consumption going back thousands of years. Emperor Jingdi of the Han dynasty, who died about 141 BCE, was buried with the plant. At first, archaeologists could only tell it was a block of plant matter, but tests showed traces of caffeine and theanine (a chemical found only in tea).

This doesn't necessarily mean people were drinking tea back then. It could have been used as medicine. But by the Tang dynasty, records show that people in China were definitely enjoying what would become the nation's favorite beverage.

The Art of Words

Chinese calligraphy is no less an art form than other forms of painting—in fact, it may be considered more important than others. There are many different varieties of calligraphy, and people value different kinds for different attributes. A simple written word can be a work of art that transcends the literal meaning of the word itself.

Skill at Chinese calligraphy takes a lot of work and practice. There are thousands of characters to learn, and each character is made up of brushstrokes that must be completed in the right order. Not only does everything have to be perfect, but artists are expected to have their own style as well! There need to be well-balanced spaces between both strokes and characters.

Chinese society expected all educated men (and some women) to be **proficient** at calligraphy. Wang Xizhi (303–361 CE) was a particularly celebrated

Chinese calligrapher. In fact, people considered some of his work to be priceless. One of his most famous works was the *Lantingxu* (or the *Lantingji Xu*), which describes a gathering of famous writers to drink wine and compose poems. The original is lost, but copies survive today.

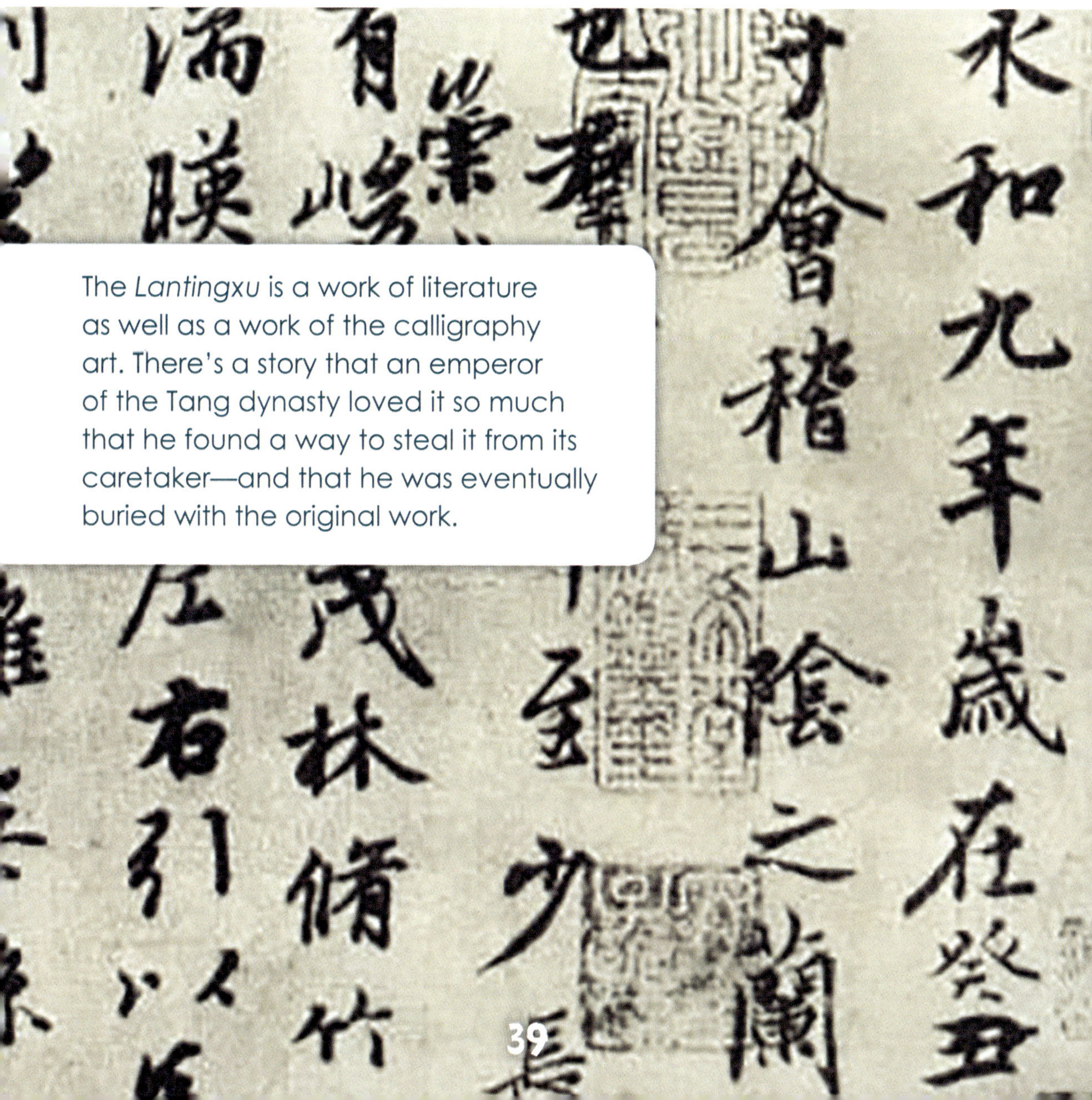

The *Lantingxu* is a work of literature as well as a work of the calligraphy art. There's a story that an emperor of the Tang dynasty loved it so much that he found a way to steal it from its caretaker—and that he was eventually buried with the original work.

Tools to grind ink, add water to ink, hold paper down, and stamp signatures are all artifacts that followed Chinese calligraphy's rise in popularity.

While some people used silk as a background for their calligraphy, some used a newer invention: paper. This medium could absorb ink in a different way than silk, and it was less expensive. People first made paper from tree bark, later adding rags and even old fishing nets to make the product stronger. The invention had far-reaching effects, especially the rise in published books.

The tools needed for Chinese calligraphy include only a brush, an ink stick, an inkstone, and paper or silk. The brush is commonly made of animal hair and is very flexible. Ink sticks are made of black ink formed into narrow shapes. They're ground against an inkstone with water to make ink again. Artists control the consistency of the ink by adjusting the amount of water versus the amount of ground ink. They also control how much ink they load on to the brush.

While there aren't many tools needed for calligraphy, the Chinese love for the art form led to even more art forms. People began to carve special seals with which to add signatures to calligraphy. They made paperweights to hold down paper, and they designed inkstones that were works of art in themselves. All these things are artifacts.

The Biggest Artifact

People built the earliest part of what's now called the Great Wall of China during the seventh to fourth centuries BCE. Emperor Qin Shi Huang had parts of the structure connected during his reign (221–210 BCE). Those of other dynasties made some repairs and added more to the wall. Then, during the late 1400s, rulers of the Ming dynasty tackled the project in earnest, creating what we think of as the Great Wall of China today.

Hundreds of thousands (maybe even millions) of people worked on the Great Wall of China while it was constructed and repaired over the centuries. These included many soldiers, common people, and convicts. While it's true that many people may have died during its construction, legends that their bodies may be buried within the wall itself have never been verified.

From about 1487 to 1505 CE, thousands of workers constructed the best-known and best-preserved section of the Great Wall, about 5,500 miles (8,851 kilometers) of fortification built of Chinese bricks, earth, and stone. Altogether, the pieces and parts of the structure stretch about 13,000 miles (20,922 km) across northern China.

Although the Great Wall no longer serves to guard against enemy troops, its very size and impressiveness continue to make it an important part of Chinese identity and culture. Today, the Great Wall of China is a national icon, a powerful symbol of the strength of ancient China—and of the power of artifacts.

The Great Wall of China is a **UNESCO** World Heritage Site. This means that the United Nations has decided that it has important cultural, historic, scientific, or other significance to the world.

Glossary

alloy Matter made of two or more metals, or a metal and a nonmetal, melted together.

Bronze Age The period in time in which people started to make bronze to make weapons and tools.

calligraphy The art of making beautiful handwriting.

diplomacy Skill in handling relationships between people or groups.

dynasty A family of rulers who control a country for a long time, or the time during a dynasty's rule.

excavate To uncover something by digging away and removing the earth that covers it.

geometric Having to do with straight lines, circles, and other simple shapes.

hilt The handle of a dagger or sword.

integrity The quality of being fair and honest.

intricate Having many parts.

leaven To add leaven, or a substance such as yeast that makes dough rise, to something.

literal Using the exact meaning of a word.

motif A design or theme that is repeated and means something.

Neolithic A time period of the late Stone Age, between the Paleolithic period and the Bronze Age.

proficient Skilled.

ritual Having to do with rites or a ritual, or an established form of a ceremony.

scabbard A case that covers a sword's blade.

subtle Hard to notice, not obvious.

tarnish To become or cause to become dull.

UNESCO The United Nations Education, Scientific, and Cultural Organization.

For More Information

Hebei Provincial Museum
4 East Street, Chang'an District
Shijiazhuang, Hebei, China
This museum has many exhibits, including the jade burial suits of Liu Sheng and Dou Wan.

Hubei Provincial Museum
No. 160, East Lake Road
Wuchang District, Wuhan
Website: www.hbww.org/home/EnglishIndex.aspx
The sword of Goujian is on display in this provincial museum.

Museum of the Terracotta Army
Lintong District
Xi'an, Shaanxi, China
Website: www.bmy.com.cn/2015new/bmyweb
Built around the excavation site itself, this museum showcases the amazing figures of the Terracotta Army.

National Museum of China
16 E Chang'an Avenue
Dongcheng District, China
Website: en.chnmuseum.cn
The National Museum of China is the second most visited museum in the world. It's run by the Ministry of Culture of China and holds many artifacts related to the country and the region.

The Smithsonian Institution
PO Box 37012
SI Building, Room 153, MRC 010
Washington, DC 20013-7012
Website: si.edu or www.si.edu/collections
Learn more about artifacts at the Smithsonian Institution, which hosts items from throughout the world.

UNESCO Headquarters
7, place de Fontenoy, 75007
Paris, France
Website: en.unesco.org
UNESCO is the United Nations Education, Scientific, and Cultural Organization. Among other things, it maintains a list of World Heritage Sites.

For Further Reading

Captivating History. *Ancient China*. Independently published: Captivating History, 2019.

Li Jian and Hou-Mei Sung. *Terracotta Army: Legacy of the First Emperor of China*. New Haven, CT: Yale University Press, 2017.

Morley, Jacqueline. *You Wouldn't Want to Work on the Great Wall of China*. New York, NY: Franklin Watts, 2017.

Nott, Stanley Charles. *Chinese Jade Throughout the Ages*. Hassell Street Press, 2021.

So, Jenny F. *Early Chinese Jades in the Harvard Art Museums*. Cambridge, MA: Harvard Art Museums, 2018.

Yang, Guimei. *Illustrated Brief History of Chinese Porcelain*. North Clarendon, VT: Tuttle Publishing, 2020.

Bibliography

Ali, Huma. "Kingfisher Feathers and the Tian-tsui Jewelry Technique." The Daily of the University of Washington. August 31, 2021. https://www.dailyuw.com/arts_and_culture/art/article_61449e56-0950-11ec-a25a-1f750d8f2c67.html.

Associated Press. "Ancient Chinese Pottery Confirmed as Oldest Yet Found." *The Guardian*. June 28, 2012. https://www.theguardian.com/science/2012/jun/28/ancient-chinese-pottery-oldest-yet.

Chang, Stephanie. "2,500-Year-Old Chinese Sword Still Looks and Cuts Like New." My Modern Met. December 8, 2016. https://mymodernmet.com/sword-of-goujian/.

China Daily. "Ancient Phoenix Crown of Sui Dynasty Unveiled in E China." September 19, 2016. http://www.chinadaily.com.cn/culture/2016-09/19/content_26827501.htm.

China Daily. "Shining Pearls at the National Museum." October 2, 2016. http://www.chinadaily.com.cn/culture/2016-10/02/content_26960791_2.htm.

Dunnell, Tony. "Sword of Goujian." Atlas Obscura. https://www.atlasobscura.com/places/sword-of-goujian.

Goran, David. "Fengguan: A Masterpiece of Traditional Chinese Jewelry." The Vintage News. December 23, 2016. https://www.thevintagenews.com/2016/12/23/fengguan-a-masterpiece-of-traditional-chinese-jewelry/.

History.com. "Great Wall of China." History Channel. November 5, 2019. https://www.history.com/topics/ancient-china/great-wall-of-china.

Hucker, C. O., et al. "China." Encyclopedia Britannica. November 2, 2021. https://www.britannica.com/place/China.

Lu, Fran. "A Tour of Beijing's National Museum of China in 20 Artefacts." CultureTrip. November 15, 2017. https://theculturetrip.com/asia/china/articles/a-tour-of-beijings-national-museum-of-china-in-20-artefacts/.

Lubow, Arthur. "Terracotta Soldiers on the March." *Smithsonian Magazine*. July 2009. https://www.smithsonianmag.com/history/terra-cotta-soldiers-on-the-march-30942673/.

Nelson, Katie. "Archaeologists Unearth the Earliest Evidence of Tea." Shanghaiist. May 5, 2018. http://shanghaiist.com/2016/01/27/earliest_tea_discovered/.

Richman-Abdou, Kelly. "The Exquisite Artistry and History of Chinese Silk Painting." My Modern Met. March 1, 2020. https://mymodernmet.com/silk-painting-history/.

Roach, John. "Emperor Qin's Tomb." *National Geographic*. https://www.nationalgeographic.com/history/article/emperor-qin.

Shan, Jun. "Importance of Jade in Chinese Culture." ThoughtCo. December 6, 2018. https://www.thoughtco.com/about-jade-culture-629197.

Silbergeld, J., Liu Qiyi, and Michael Sullivan. "Chinese Painting." Encyclopedia Britannica. November 1, 2021. https://www.britannica.com/art/Chinese-painting.

Song, Candace. "The Terracotta Army: A Complete Guide." China Highlights. October 11, 2021. https://www.chinahighlights.com/xian/terracotta-army/.

Tan, Kenneth. "YUM! Archaeologists Discover That People in Xinjiang Were Snacking on Dumplings 1,700 Years Ago." Shanghaiist. May 5, 2018. http://shanghaiist.com/2016/02/15/1700_year_old_dumplings_found_in_xinjiang/.

Walansky, Aly. "The Ancient Chinese Were Just as Obsessed with Dumplings as We Are." *Food & Wine*. June 29, 2017. https://www.foodandwine.

Index